LOOK MOM!
NO PAIN!

A cancer warrior's walk through pain, tears, laughter, and amazing grace

Toni Brown

ISBN: 979-8-9879955-4-9

Published by:
Novel Prose Publishing

Cover and interior design: Lisa R. Perron – lisa@lisarperron.com

Endless thanks to my niece, Lisa Perron. Without your love, knowledge, and skills in gathering, organizing, printing, and publishing, our dreams of sharing Toni's heart with the reader could not have come true. Thank you, Lisa. Toni loved you, and so do I.

These are my days. These are not cancer's days; they are mine, and I will seize them!! Carpe Diam, everyone. I love you!
Thank you for holding me up!

Toni Brown

FORWARD

Toni was my daughter, my best friend, my confidant, and soulmate. We traveled together through her five-year journey with cancer, one day at a time and moment by moment.

Toni was diagnosed with colon cancer in 2017. After surgery and several rounds of chemo, there was no evidence of remaining cancer. She hoped that that was the end of that! Her infusion port was removed, and life was good again. She saw no need to journal her experience at this time or to share it with others. As we know too well with cancer, this is not always the case. When it did return, she joined an online colon cancer support group, hoping to find someone to share her thoughts and fears with that could totally understand them.

Feeling the support from this group, Toni was inspired to share her journey with cancer on social media. Having a deep, simple faith, she knew that prayer was what was going to be needed to give her the strength to walk this daunting road. We gathered all her prayer warriors, and off she went, achieving her deep desire to share her joys and struggles honestly, hoping and praying it would help others to walk whatever path they were on today! Her gratitude for all her warriors was immeasurable.

Toni's mom.
Mary Whitaker

PREFACE

First off, I am by no means a writer. My family and friends have been encouraging me to write in the hopes that my journey can help someone else. I have been somewhat journaling on Facebook since my diagnosis in January of 2017, sharing glimpses of my journey to my amazing family and tribe of Prayer Warriors. I am hoping that this will not be a sad story but one of enlightenment for future fighters and caregivers. We learn as we move through this horrible disease, and if my story can help someone else move through this easier, then I will forever be grateful that I wrote this.

If you are reading this, then I know your life has been affected by this tragic disease. Please know that I understand. I am already praying for you, I get you, and I am so sorry that you have to go through this! Please know that you are not alone. There are many of us! Let's fight this battle together!

THE BEGINNING—MY DISEASE

In 2016, I was misdiagnosed in the emergency room with Crohn's Disease. I had a CT scan that was clouded by some kind of abdominal infection, and the tumor could not be seen. My symptoms were exactly the same as Crohn's, and the gastro doctor on call recommended that I get a colonoscopy and put me on prednisone. He also explained that because I had no insurance, I could not be seen at his office! Did you hear that? It was up to me to figure out how to find someone to treat me and how to pay for an expensive procedure. He was a total jerk! Had he admitted me to the hospital that day, the colonoscopy would have been done immediately. He tossed that idea around, got a phone call, and left. The nurse discharged me soon after.

I was also under the care of a great group of Direct Care Doctors. They too looked at the cloudy CT scan and thought his diagnosis was on target, but strongly recommended I get a colonoscopy. I, the frugal, broke hairdresser, decided to go with this diagnosis and treat it as such, taking prednisone for seventy-six days—not a good thing to say the least. My symptoms never decreased, and my aunt sent me the money for the colonoscopy. We drove to a different city to have the procedure as the cash price was less expensive than my hometown price. That day was the beginning of my cancer diagnosis. I can't remember that doctor's name. I wish I could; he was very nice and concerned when he discovered I had a tumor, so concerned that he tattooed it for surgery and called me two days later with the pathology. I was with a customer when he said the word cancer to me. "We can't wait," he said, "and start weaning off the prednisone immediately!" I believe that drug had been feeding that illusive tumor for seventy-six days.

Surgery was quick, with the removal of a section of my lower colon and some reconstruction to my bladder as there was so much scar tissue from previous surgeries and that crazy infection. The surgeon said the tumor was days away from rupturing and asked if I had a high pain tolerance. I laughed. I've been moving through various stages of pain most of my adult life. Stuff happens, you know, broken bones, illness, heartache; I always choose to move through these things. You know, pull up your bootstraps and keep going! Great attitude—bad idea for this situation!

This was the first of many HUGE lessons for me. Always listen to your body! I truly believe our bodies tell us what it needs. Please don't ignore it ever; it speaks to us every day. If your thirsty, hydrate. If you crave asparagus, eat it. If it needs to move, move it! And always tell a medical professional if you are symptomatic. I had previous symptoms for years that I explained away as common. I did NOT have a colonoscopy at 50 as recommended. Had I done that, this cancer would have probably been caught as a polyp and never metastasized to other parts of my body.

Everything else from that point forward is kind of hazy. Dates are gone from my brain. It was a crazy whirlwind of accepting this diagnosis of cancer, knowing it affected some lymph glands already, telling my daughter and friends and family. Meeting my amazing cancer doctor, getting a plan for chemo, having a port for the chemo surgically put in place, promising clients that I loved dearly that I would soon return, thinking at the time that it may be possible to work some through chemo on my *good days*. That was never to happen.

I didn't journal on Facebook at that time because I was going to handle all of this privately, telling only close family and friends. I was going to move through this as I did everything in my life and add it to the rest of my stories of hope among adversity. Read on; that quickly changes.

FACEBOOK

March 25, 2017

Every time I get worried, I look at this and think how blessed I am to have so many prayer warriors. If I haven't thanked you in person, I thank you now! I don't know where I would be without you all!!!

September 10, 2017

Anxiously awaiting my LAST chemo treatment—reflecting on the journey thus far. It's been rough for sure, but I am so hopeful that my future holds exciting new adventures!! I'm already working to create and share beautiful things! Thank you, prayer warriors! I could not have survived without YOU!! Please continue to pray. I have a lot of healing to do physically, mentally, emotionally, and spiritually, but I am up for the task. And, also pray that the prayers and medicine worked we definitely can't forget that!! One more and done!!

July 30, 2018

So, I haven't posted much on Facebook about my health because I don't want my prayer warriors to worry, but I think maybe I could use you all right now!! I don't believe it's serious, but my last CT was a little sketchy with some crap in my lungs. I took some antibiotics, and I felt better for a month or so. Yesterday's CT shows more crap in my lungs than before, nodules that haven't changed, blah blah blah. The good news is that it could be some kind of crazy infection that the antibiotics didn't fix. I'm seeing a pulmonologist tomorrow at 11:00 am. I'm sure there will be more tests, but geez, this is nerve wracking. Please pray for my sanity and for a good resolution for this! Thank you all for loving me and praying for me! You give me comfort beyond belief!

July 31, 2018

Update: Good news! We are treating this as an infection for now because the nodules haven't changed in three months. He believes it is unlikely cancer, but of course, that can't be ruled out. Another CT scan in six months. Yay! Lol. I am to call him ASAP if there are any changes, or I don't get better. I felt very taken care of. As to smoking, I know you're all thinking about it. I know it's something I need to work on, and I plan to do that. He didn't berate me or even tell me I had to quit. He just wants me to slowly work toward lessening the need for them, timing them and stretching it out as far as I can, and to keep my stress level down. I almost kissed him!! He totally gets how hard it is, and I didn't feel like a total piece of crap when I left. It makes it easier to want to when someone is not telling you that you have to! Thanks for all your prayers. I plan to get better soon and rock this world for a longgggg, longgggg time!

July 31, 2018

So, I've had a few minutes to process all the medical events of the last few days. I truly believe that all the love and prayer and good wishes changed the outcome for me today! I truly believe that. I told my mom tonight that I skated on a devastating battle that I was so scared to fight!! I feel so grateful—so blessed and so loved. Thank you all so much!! If anyone of you ever need me, please reach out privately on Facebook or whatever. I'm here for you no matter what.

October 20, 2018

Feeling so peaceful. Trusting and letting go are hard things for me, and the world sure is noisy! It's been a while since I've felt like myself, but I'm thinking, I'm getting ME back, and I'm at peace today, loving and trusting myself! That's a really great feeling!

November 6, 2018

This morning, I'm thinking about cancer, not in a bad way, but with love for all of my fellow fighters!! Wishing I could explain to the world what we go through mentally, spiritually, physically, and emotionally. We live with our swords drawn, always waiting to fight the next battle if it comes for us. We live in fear of test results because we don't want to have to be sick anymore. We just don't! We live with the side effects of the horrible medicine our bodies have already had to endure! We fight daily for our health and worry about what this has done to our family and friends. We don't want them to have to go through any of this!! We don't!! And we walk in this world with grace and thanksgiving for another day. I know I do anyway. So to all my fellow warriors, I say this: I get you. I love you. And I hope you have an amazing day. Carpe Diem!!

December 11, 2018

Okay prayer warriors, I think it's time to circle the wagons again. I'm sorry to say, the last bloodwork six weeks ago showed an elevation in my tumor markers, but we watch it and if it goes up, it shows a possible occurrence. This time it's up considerable. I'm gonna have another CT scan ASAP, but not sure when. I'll keep you posted! Scary, but I'm okay. Feeling good and at peace for whatever is to come. "Battle on" is my new motto!! Love you all!

December 19, 2018

So, I promised to keep you all posted. CT scan is tomorrow and results on Friday. Thank you all for the kind words and prayers!! I always feel so blessed to know that so many love me and are raising me up for healing. I'm feeling good and positive! Had a wonderful week with some of the best people imaginable. Hoping for nothing, but if it is something, I also know I've got a good fighting spirit, and I'll rock it just like last time!! I'll be sure and update as soon as I know anything. Love you all!

A Warrior is Born

December 21, 2018

As promised, but not good news I'm so sorry to say. CT showed a spot in my liver and one in my lung. I'm not surprised about the lung one because we have been watching an abnormality for six months. It grew quite a bit, spent a lot of time with my amazing Dr. C. He called a specialist at KU Med, and we are working on a good plan. Tentative plan is a few chemo treatments then a couple of surgeries to remove those little tumors, then probably more chemo. It's not good news but workable at this point. I'm exhausted, but I know that I have the strength in me to fight this battle! I told my mom I feel like a soldier going to war. I'm ready for a battle, chin up, back straight, sword drawn, facing this horrible disease head on! Knowing that I have so many people who love me makes this so much easier. I truly love you all!

January 29, 2019

Kinda told my story today to someone who is now dear to me, and I've been feeling really pissed off all over again about this damn disease and myself really. This could have been prevented if I had not blown off symptoms that I had for a couple of years! I couldn't afford insurance. I was too busy taking care of everyone else and couldn't take time off work. It's okay. I can live with it. Selfless me, right? No! Please, people, if I can give you one piece of wisdom or advice I would say this, please, please, please if you are symptomatic even in the least see a doctor. It's so easy. I wish I would have handled this disease before it handled me! I can't turn back the clock, but as Smokey the Bear said, "Only you can prevent forest fires." Colon cancer, I believe, is almost epidemic! In just one private group I'm in, at least ten new members a day and we are 11,500 strong, and many are under 30 with stage four cancer!

March 22, 2019

I am home. Surgery didn't go as planned—another detour as they found a few more jelly like tumors (I can't remember what he called them) in my abdomen. New plan is to go to KU Med. There is a surgeon there that may be able to do a chemo wash to destroy those and remove the tumor on my liver and lung all at the same time. So, I recover from this one and start over there. Dr. Hamilton was pretty excited about this as he knows patients that responded really well to this treatment.

So disappointed and really tired, but my tribe of prayer warriors will get me through. Thank you all!! I will keep you posted.

March 28, 2019

Just letting you guys know that I have an appointment at KU Med next Wednesday with a surgical oncologist. I have been doing a little research as to what may be in my future physically. I've been walking and trying to get out every day since surgery last Friday. Gotta get strong from the last surgeries, so I can be as healthy as I can be for what's coming up. Not gonna lie right now, I'm tired— worried—scared—and just plain disgusted with this whole mess. I know this funk will pass, but you guys raising me up always makes me feel better!! Thank you all!! I love you!

April 2, 2019

Here's what we learned at KU Med today. Hope I can articulate it right. My colon cancer has thrown off lots of little tumors that attach to the outside of organs. If it was in my blood, it would attack the inside. That's why chemo didn't work. Pathology shows cancerous spots in my abdominal wall as well as my liver. Because I am relatively healthy with no other medical issues, I'm a great candidate for a pretty invasive procedure, where he removes all visible cancer in my abdomen, including all of the little tumors waiting to attach to something and washes all of my organs with chemo for sixty to ninety minutes. That surgery is scheduled for April 19th, Good Friday!! Which I believe in my heart is the right day. This is gonna be rough and painful with at least three days in ICU and ten days to two weeks at best in the hospital, and that is with no complications. Feeding tube probably and a long recovery. But I feel grateful and HOPEFUL. I truly believe all past roads have led to this moment! I don't wanna, but I'm gonna go because the hope of having time…lots of it makes me giddy.

April 17, 2019

Hey gang, I found out today that the pesky spot in my lung wants to raise its ugly head again. Remember, we've been chasing this thing for almost a year. I don't believe it's cancer (I could be in denial), but in order to do the other surgery on Friday, we have to get rid of this too, so we just added another surgery to the overwhelmingly amount of stuff my body is going to go through. Scary for me to say the least, but I'm not scared I'm going to die!! I need everyone to know that I'm just scared of the pain and recovery! IT WILL BE OKAY! I know this in my heart. I have so much faith in the fact that I'm taken care of all the time.

April 20, 2019

Mary Whitaker

I promised Toni that I would let you all know that surgery is over, and all went the very best we could have expected. What a treacherous and amazing procedure!! And the tumor they removed from her lung had no cancer cells! Amazing news!! I am staying with her tonight. They are having a hard time trying to catch up with her pain. It will be a long, hard revovery, but you know Toni!! She can do it!! Thanks to everyone for all your prayers and great thoughts. God is so Good!

April 22, 2019

Mary Whitaker is with **Toni Brown**

Just an update—they have moved Toni out of ICU. They explained this morning that because of the chemo wash she had, the next few days will be rough for her, and then she will begin to feel better. Thanks again for all your prayers. Keep them going, please.

May 3, 2019

Mary Whitaker is with **Toni Brown**.

It hasn't been a great week for Toni, but we are home to recover! She is staying with us for now. Please feel free to come see her here. A friendly face is sometimes just what the doctor ordered! Just let us know. She will see the doctor at KU on the 15th to have staples removed, etc. God has been good. Keep up those prayers!!

May 30, 2019

Every morning if it's even remotely sunny, I sneak out my parent's back door and bask in the morning sun, listening to the breeze in the trees and the birds doing their morning chirping. It's beautiful and peaceful! I struggle with patience and the sheer slowness of this healing process, but I am grounded safe in my parent's home, so well taken care of and loved! I wanna go home, take care of myself, sit on my own porch, but it's not time yet, and I'm okay with that. I'm truly grateful to be alive today and so looking forward to what the future holds! Hope you all enjoy this glorious day!

June 7, 2019

I am constantly reminding myself to be patient. It will come! I have never been a person to lie down for so long. This healing process has been so damn slow and frustrating and mostly just annoying. Planning to go home in a couple days, and I'm afraid. Fearless me is afraid. Afraid I can't handle taking care of myself. Good grief, that sounds ridiculous doesn't it. My ever-loving mom will be right up the road. Slapping myself in the head this morning and reminding myself that God has a plan for me. He didn't bring me through this just to let me fail or dangle in fear. It's okay. I'm okay. Everything will be okay. Thank you all again for your constant support and for reading my silly morning self-talk!

June 14, 2019

Good morning, everyone. Here's the good, joyful news this morning. Three weeks ago, I had bloodwork to check for active tumors. They are now checking it with three different tests. One was as low as it's ever been, and the other two were high—above normal. I have literally been holding my breath for my recheck on Wednesday and the good news is they are also coming down nicely!! Whewwww. It's hard to hold your breath for three weeks!! Lol. Every emotion I have ever had about this disease and this crazy surgery came rushing out of me in one huge wave: relief!!! This fighting cancer job is the hardest thing I have ever done. Now maybe I'll get a reprieve. Maybe this whole excruciating surgery will have been worth it. Maybe I can live cancer free for a while and heal and relax and find a happy balance! I'm so excited. I think I'll go home and practice taking care of myself. I'm getting better, really, and for that, I'm truly grateful!!! I love you all!! Have a great weekend!

June 18, 2019

Awe, from my dad—anti-depression
wildflowers picked right out of his field!! Love
them and him!

June 23, 2019

ONE DAY, YOU
WILL TELL
YOUR STORY
OF HOW
YOU'VE
OVERCOME
WHAT YOU'RE
GOING
THROUGH NOW,
AND IT WILL
BECOME PART
OF SOMENE
ELSE'S
SURVIVAL
GUIDE.

I believe that all of our suffering and pain are to help guide the ones who come after us, to show them their own strength through our struggles. I pray to always be open to being an instrument to others who suffer and may feel alone. My story is not a new one, but I feel it's important to tell.

July 7, 2019

Oh, the magnificent stars!! Og Mandino wrote a book that literally changed my life when I was young and made me realize how incredibly made we are and how beautiful life can be! I love the memory of that book!

CHEMOTHERAPY

I saw a 30-year-old girl in the cancer center the other day, having her first treatment of the first chemotherapy medicines that I started with. I'm on my third round and have had multiple surgeries at this point for metastasis. I wanted to reach out, to hug her, but I didn't. It's shocking the first day of treatment—how immediate the side effects are—how damn scary it is! You go in feeling relatively healthy, and in a matter of hours, you are pale, queasy, dizzy, and symptomatic. Her family was with her, and she was brave.

> Webster's definition of brave: having or showing mental or moral strength to face danger, fear or difficulty: having or showing courage.

I was her three years ago. I am her today. I didn't hug her or engage her because I didn't want to let my cancer story steal her hope. I hugged her with my heart and prayed that this one round of fighting for her would be her CURE!!

Chemo drugs are a double-edged sword. I look at it like this: we are fighting fire with fire, meaning these life-saving drugs are meant to KILL this disease. The healthy parts of our bodies must endure the onslaught of these drugs coursing through them. Yes, there are extreme side effects—vomiting, nausea, diarrhea, neuropathy, hair loss, and the list goes on. Those are the physical side effects. Some of the worst for me are the mental ones: anxiety, panic, depression, fear, and confusion. I'm here to tell you CHEMO BRAIN is REAL!! Let me say that again; CHEMO BRAIN is REAL!

Here's the good news. Most of these side effects, in my case anyway, pass right around day five or six after treatment. Hold on to that knowledge and repeat it to yourself 1000 times a day.

FACEBOOK

July 11, 2019

So, I had my first scan yesterday after this monumental surgery, and I didn't get very good news. I now have a tumor on my adrenal gland above my right kidney. Still working out the details of what this entails, maybe biopsy, maybe chemo, maybe a trial at KU Med. I wasn't going to tell you all because I didn't want you to think your prayers aren't working. I would never want that! I so hoped that I would get some time between battles, but this disease is a sneaky, evil, horrible thing and it mutates at will. I knew that! I was just hoping for some time. What I would invite you all to do is to continue to pray for strength for me to fight yet again because, well I need it. I'm not yet healed from the last few go arounds, but I'm working hard, I promise, and will be ready for whatever comes my way!! Love you bunches!!

August 5, 2019

Haha! How I handled this day!! It always amazes me how something big breaks or needs to be tended to right before I have to tend to my health, the car this time, two trips to the shop, lots of money, and we are still driving my mom's car to KU Med to meet a new doc and try to get a plan for future treatment!! Ugh. But don't you worry. I'm good at this problem-solving stuff, and life is just too darn short to sweat the small stuff, so we celebrated my girl's birthday at Olive Garden and put all the stress of this day away!!

August 6, 2019

I know some of you are wondering what we heard at KU Med. Chemo will start up again here in Topeka soon, not sure when, but the same chemo as last time, just dialed down a little, so maybe I'm not so sick. If my tumor markers continue to go up we will switch to two other drugs and see what we get out of that. If that doesn't work, lol, (cuz you have to have humor!!) they are just starting a trial on my specific kind of genetic cancer that may be an option in the future. My head is swimming, but I am in good hands.

August 12, 2019

Today I went to Barnes and Noble to look for a book. What I found there was a boy who was talking to the manager asking him to call someone because he was suicidal—in the bookstore. The manager handled it well! He tried his mom and then 911. I hovered listening, and my heart broke a little. I wanted to hug him, heal his pain, but some young employee was gently talking to him when I left. I feel so proud of her and grateful that they handled him in a respectful responsible way!! I shed a tear for him and pray that he got the help he needs. There is so much of this today. Please if you see someone in real distress, stay safe, but do what you can. Make that call!

August 21, 2019

August 28, 2019

THE TREES ARE ABOUT TO SHOW US HOW LOVELY IT IS TO LET THINGS GO.

Letting go of anything my whole entire life has been a real challenge for me. Fighting battles for outcomes that don't come is the worst! I want to try harder, do it all better, and get a better result. I didn't ever realize I was so competitive in this game called life, but I'm practicing letting go.

August 26, 2019

So, I snuck a little peak at my cat scan results
from Friday as I don't have a doctor's
appointment until next week. I've been really
holding my breath about a couple of issues.
The good news is nothing has changed or
grown!! No new tumors! Stable, stable, stable!!
I breathed a huge sigh of relief. I'm chemo
sick, but I will feel better in a day or two. I
feel hopeful again that we are staying ahead of
this and that these treatments are going to
keep this disease at bay! It's crazy what your
mind tries to do to your hope and strength
while under the influence of these life-saving
meds. Chemo brain is so real, and for me it
looks like anxiety and fear and confusion, but
it does pass, and I know it! It's so important
to have a plan for keeping my mind right, so I
don't' get swept away in the fog. Good news,
quiet meditation, and redirecting my thoughts
always helps!! Today is going to be a good
day!

September 2, 2019

I've gotta tell you, friends, I've spent the last few days feeling loved beyond measure!! Sometimes during this journey of treatments and tests and surgeries, I kinda get to a point where I'm beyond tired and want to quit. This fight is hard. And then these beautiful days happen, and I'm strengthened by my amazing family and friends and really know in my heart that quitting is not an option!! You guys are truly my armor. You raise my sword. You give me purpose and love, and for that, I am forever grateful!

September 15, 2019

Awe. And I still feel the same today!! Thanks for being the rock that I cling to!

From September 15, 2014:

Dear Mom. I think you're amazing! Thank you for being a light in my life! I love you to the moon and back. Just saying it out loud for the millionth time.

October 9, 2019

For those of you who don't know, I had a little issue Monday that landed me in the hospital. Apparently, all the surgeries and chemo have led me to a small intestine obstruction. Pretty painful stuff!! We are hoping to fix it non-surgically in the next few days, so I'm having a nice stay at St. Francis Hospital. Just wanted all my friends and warriors to know. I'll keep you posted.

October 12, 2019

I'm still enjoying my beautiful stay at St. Francis Hospital!! Joking. But I'm getting good care! Looks like I will be here at least until Monday. Going to maybe let me try some clear liquids today. Dr. C says chemo is the culprit for the bowel to swell, and it seems to be taking care of itself so far. I'm so ready to bust out of here, but I guess I better stay put.

October 15, 2019

I woke up this morning feeling joyful and blessed! Quickly made my grocery list and headed to the store!! These thoughts have been rolling through my head all day. The only way I am going to recover from laying in a hospital bed for a week is to move, to move physically, to move mentally, to move spiritually! To go out and practice being me!! If I could encourage anyone dealing with anything chronically, I would say this: keep moving. Resist the chains that want to debilitate. Don't cave to the negative thoughts that want to keep us down. On our worst days, we must still try to move even if it's in the most minimal of ways. We are tougher than we think and stronger than we think and can do more than we think. We are blessed! Maybe not with good health today, but with sooooo many other things, look for them, search them out and count them!! My mantra for this will be Carpe Diem. Seize the day!! Love you all. Thank you so much for who you are to me!!

October 22, 2019

Tomorrow will be a week since I returned to
the hospital for surgery. Yes, I'm still here,
healing nicely and slowly adding food to my
diet of IV goodies. We decided to go slow and
not try to rush home this time, hoping this
will prevent any relapse. I'm terribly bored
and really missing my Louie, but I'm feeling
better and trying to be a good patient. LOL!
So, just thought some of you may e
wondering what's been going on and that's it
in a happy little nutshell.

October 26, 2019

I finally made it HOME! Seventeen days of October spent as an inpatient at St. Francis was enough for this chick! I'm feeling good, and we think once I recover from this surgery, I'm going to feel better than I have in many months. Tons of scar tissue removed from the major surgery I had in April was the culprit. Thanks to everyone who visited, texted, called, prayed, and checked up on me. I am truly blessed, and I love you all!!

NEGATIVE EMOTION

Fear, resentment, jealousy, anger, and self-pity. Those are the monsters that rear their ugly head in my mind. They get to playing around in there, and some days control my whole thought process. I don't feed them or entertain them much anymore. They are not guided by God.

Those demons want to get in the way of love, peace, contentment, and joy. They are powerful! They want me to stay in the dark and play their little games.

I don't think many of us know that we can stop this process and control the sad, dark, emotions within us. How could we if we were not taught to? If we grew up watching someone else ride the roller coaster of negative emotions, watched them crisis manage their lives and everyone else's? We learned that we were responsible to these dark thoughts and *had* to entertain them. Like the relative that no one likes, but we invite them to dinner anyway out of sheer duty.

Our duty is not to feel the dark for ourselves or anyone else. Period. Those thoughts breed insecurity, self-doubt, and depression. Who could possibly achieve their goals and desires wrapped up in those feelings? No one that I've ever met.

Today, I am committed to letting the demons go. They are not friends of mine! I do not want them at my dinner party! I will keep telling them to go away until they actually go away.

Prayer: Dear Lord, thank you for bringing me these thoughts and words today. Help me to free myself of insecurity and self-doubt, so that I may truly become who YOU want me to be. Amen.

MEMORIES

Memories don't just bring
pictures in our minds of times past.
They bring the feelings with them.

Memories lurk and sneak
into our thoughts
blindsiding us and returning
us to the past.

Memories remind us
of the good and bad,
of the times we want again
and
the times we wish we never had.

Memories show us pictures
of our lives.
What we want to see
and
what we want to hide.

Memories are haunting
and daunting.
Choosing whether to bring
pleasure or pain.

Memories connect
the heart and the mind
with emotions of the past
to the heart of today.

I bet you've had this happen:
memories slammed into the side of my head
like a car wreck today. Overwhelming me with
emotion, good and bad. Reminding me of
things I used to have. My heart must finish
grieving the past so my soul can find peace
with it. I miss the good and hate the bad. I
want to look back with fondness, not pain,
with acceptance, not loss, with gratitude, not
hate.

Prayer: Dear Lord, I give thanks to you today
for all of my experiences, good and bad. I
trust that You were always holding my hand.
Please continue to do so as I move through
this time. Help me to accept with love that I
am right where You mean me to be. Amen.

SEPARATION

When she comes to terms with
all the bad feelings in her world,
she comes to terms with separating
from how these feelings feel.

There's no hate in her heart.
She has never worn that well.
Hate would kill her spirit and
send her straight to hell.

This separation is knowing that
sometimes feelings steal.
She must choose to rise above them
So she can see what's real.

Letting go of bad emotion
is something she must do.
Protecting of herself,
must be key to her.

She will be a better woman,
and all things will fall in place
if she gracefully let's go
So she can see HIS face.

(2021) I've been working on writing and re-writing this poem because emotions change with the tide, but it always ends in my love and desire to be closer to my maker—always, every time—this world is hard, and I'm so grateful to have this faith.

TOGETHER

As I wander around, looking for the light
my mind wants to be filled with the emotion
of fright.
The voice said, "Keep looking; it's just up
ahead.
You must trust the direction you're led."

"Are you sure?" I said, "This place looks
awfully bleak.
It's cold out there, and I don't have enough
heat.

The voice said, "Keep moving, dear one.
I promise I will warm you with my sun.
This is a new day, and it's only just begun."

"Yes," I said, although I forgot my scarf.
"It's not so bad as I move away from the
dark."
I was warmed completely, and my senses
engaged.
Sights, sound, and beauty permeated my
brain.

The voice said, "Now, isn't that better?
You've been warmed by my spirit,
and we will always do this together.

FACEBOOK

November 1, 2019

I know mine are!!!

November 2, 2019

There is a purpose for everyone you meet. Some people come into your life to test you, some to teach you, some to use you, and some bring out the very best in you.

I value all these people, but seriously folks, it's way better to walk in this world as a blessing than a lesson!! Be kind. Be gentle. Be loving. Be giving. Be honest. That's the golden key to this world we live in.

November 3, 2019

This morning, I'm thinking about cancer, not in a bad way, but with love for all my fellow fighters!! Wishing I could explain to the world what we go through mentally, spiritually, physically, and emotionally. We live with our swords drawn, aways waiting to fight the next battle if it comes for us! We live in fear of test results because we don't want to have to be sick anymore—we just don't!! We live with the side effects of the horrible medicine our bodies have already had to endure! We fight daily for our health and worry about what this has done to our family and friends. We don't want them to have to go through any of this! We don't!! And we walk in this world with grace and thanksgiving for another day. I know I do anyway. So, to all my fellow warriors, I say this: I get you. I love you. And I hope you have an amazing day. Carpe diem!!

November 3, 2019

Today has been such an emotional day for me. I've been following my new friend Steve Sodergren on his journey of his 50th marathon, fighting for cancer, taking us fighters, survivors, and those we lost with him. I am struggling to get better, feel like there is no time to waste, looking for some deep strength to raise me up! This shit takes its toll on me in a monumental way, physically, mentally, emotionally, and spiritually. It's such a battle all day, every day, and then there is people like Steve who walk the walk with us, and I truly know that we are the reason he ran to the finish line of his 50th marathon in all this great nation's states! Wow. What determination and dedication and what a heart of gold he has. He truly gets it!! Today I felt his strength and am determined to battle on!! Thank you, Steve. I needed this today!! Congratulations on this great accomplishment!! I love New York!! You rock, and I am blessed to meet you!!

November 6, 2019

Hi there!! I know that I am a visual thinker
and tend to picture things in a certain way. I
have often wondered how you all think I look
after some monumental health issue or when
you know I am doing battle with this disease.
I just want to assure you that my body is an
amazing fighting machine and although I look
like death "literally" at certain times, I am a
healer and am so grateful for how I can get
from there to here in the most amazing ways!!
Feeling great and ready to rock whatever life
throws my way!! Love you all!! Thanks for
holding me up. I just wanted you all to see
that I'm okay.

November 9, 2019

IF SOMEONE GAVE YOU A
BOX OF EVERYTHING YOU
HAVE EVER LOST, WHAT IS
THE FIRST THING YOU WILL
LOOK FOR?

Oh boy. This is deep. Not sure I would even look in that box. I prefer to look for blessings in what I have today.

November 14, 2019

Geez, I can't believe my eighteen days of freedom and healing are almost over!! Monday at 8:20 am, I get back into the cancer fighting game and back in the chemo chair. I'm not looking forward to it, but I'm gonna do it! I believe that this course of treatment was working pretty well and am looking forward to it continuing to do so. Not feeling completely healed from the last surgery, and my energy level is in the toilet, but I'm trying to be hopeful that I will get back to my spry self some day.

Say some prayers for me, would ya, please. I'm feeling the darkness of all this wanting to steal my joy and am mad at myself cuz I still have three good days, and I'm wasting my time in the dumps. Thank you, Warriors. I know you have my back. Cancer sucks. Chemo sucks. We have to keep fighting!

November 14, 2019

My Louie's don't you ever leave me again
face!! Haha. I do believe he missed me.
Grumpy Halloween kitty!

November 20, 2019

I've been writing this post in my head all day
after a convo with my cancer doc's nurse
practitioner about cancer patients and how
much loss we endure. It was really surreal
because it all flashed before my eyes—the
loss—the pain—the fear. I have been through
a LOT. But, here is what I said to her,
something along these lines. We can mourn
those losses, as we should, but we cannot stay
there. Carrying that around is more
detrimental to our health than anything else
we could do to ourselves. We cannot become
victims to this terrible disease!! If we do, it
wins. We lose our will to fight! A couple days
ago, I was a mess—sick, tired, hurting,
helpless, and hopeless for a minute. 'Til I
slapped myself in the forehead!! Lol. Literally
told myself to change my mindset. Change
your thinking. This too shall pass. It works, I
promise, and keeps me moving forward. I got
good news today. Tumor markers are down to
two. No chemo 'til the 18th. I have time to
heal!! I praised Jesus right there in her office! I

cried relieved joyful tears, and I owe it all to you. Thank you, Warriors!

November 25, 2019

Prayer of St. Francis

Lord, make me an instrument
of your peace;
Where there is hatred, let me sow love;
Where there is injury, pardon;
Where there is doubt, faith;
Where there is despair, hope;
Where there is darkness, light;
And where there is sadness, joy.

O Divine Master,
Grant that I may not so much seek
to be consoled as to console;
To be understood as to understand;
To be loved as to love.
For it is in giving that we receive;
It is in pardoning that we are pardoned;
And it is in dying that
we are born to eternal life.

Drove around for a while listening to the radio really loud and looking for some beauty and inspiration in this world around me. Life gets hard sometimes, and I don't always wake up with good purpose a plan to fill my day and keep my mind right.

December 15, 2019

Chemo anxiety is so real, you would think
after all this time it would be like going to
work, just something you gotta do, and I do
that most of the time. I know this is a battle
that has to be fought but the night before,
ugh, knowing that I'm going to be suffering
again for days in a fog, fatigued, and
nauseous—not being able to go love on my
people. It sucks in a huge way, and tonight
I'm feeling a little sorry for myself! Please pray
for strength for me! I hope I don't do this
every two weeks, but I can't promise that. Lol.
You all give me purpose and hope, and for
that I am sooooo grateful.

December 16, 2019

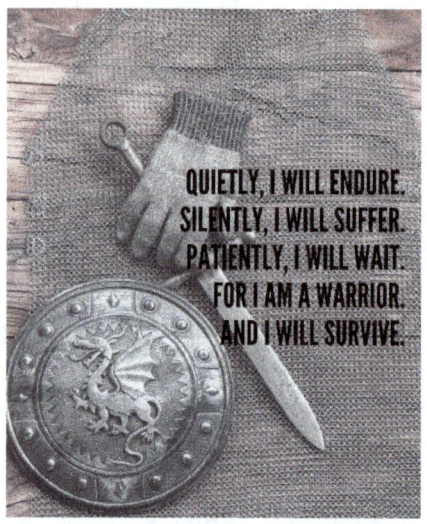

So, I got my ass up and here this morning!! Feeling strong! Thanks to my prayer warriors. I truly feel you surrounding me!! I promise I will rock this treatment just like the rest of them!! Love you guys!

December 18, 2019

> **Courage** is knowing it
> might hurt and doing it
> anyway.
>
> **Stupidity** is the same.
>
> And that's why life is hard.
>
> JEREMY GOLDBERG

So being chemo sick, I find this ironic and soooo true. Which am I? #chemo sucks, and cancer is stupid!! And that's all I have to say about that!

JOURNALING

I don't think I've explained why I
write the words that I do, words that move
me on a particular day. I read from three or
four daily meditations and land on the one
that speaks to me. I read it a few times then
write my thoughts. I do this so the words will
imprint themselves into my brain, so I can use
them as tools later or to form my attitude for
the day. Part of letting go of past behavior
and need is to form new habits and new
beliefs, to practice these things until they
become me, to practice a more positive self-
talk until it pushes out the old *stinking thinking*.
It works! I promise! Be gentle with yourself
though; it's a process. Habits of behavior that
took a lifetime to form don't go away easily,
even if they are wrong. That's why I pray for
acceptance and patience. I used to pray for
things to change in someone else, so I could
finally be happy. Now I pray for things to

change within myself, so that I may be FREE to be happy.

I am learning that happiness truly does come from within and even though this *work* on myself is a slow process, it's much quicker and more satisfying than trying to change the world! Ha, like I have that power, right? So, for now, I read, I pray, and I write my way to a better me.

Prayer: Dear Lord, I give thanks to you today for giving me clarity, for giving me acceptance, for giving me patience. I may pray for it again tomorrow, but today I will own it! Amen.

FACEBOOK

December 22, 2019

I've been preparing for this amazing holiday
and feeling a little blue, trying to remember
last year and feeling confused. Why was last
year stressful? Then I recall a bad scan and a
call from the surgeon on Christmas Eve. Port
placement is scheduled the 26th. I thought I
was done with this crap. It's been an
extremely crazy year big surgeries and so
much worry about my health, loads of painful
recovery, but I know if it wasn't for that
surgeon more than once and my doctors and
all of you prayer warriors, things could be
much different! I'm counting my blessings
tonight in a big way. I get a chemo break until
January 6th and am looking forward to
celebrating with family and friends! Love you
all!! Thanks for holding me up!

January 5, 2020

Had an extra week off chemo, and today is the first day I have felt myself, lol. That's how it goes, woke up clear-headed with loads of energy!! It's been a long three weeks. But I am grateful for them! I've been busy seeing all my people and loved ones. It's so important to keep moving whether I "feel like it or not." I know that and I do that! Blessings always come to me when I push through the fatigue and fog! I always feel a little anxiety when it's time to saddle up again, but I'm gonna do it like I always do it! Say a little prayer for me. I hate chemo, but I'm gonna go. Love you guys, and I know you're holding me up!!

January 6, 2020

This!!

January 15, 2020

I'm better!! Whoop, whoop! Last week was bad--worse than bad--like throw in the towel, I'm not doing this anymore bad. I apparently acquired a respiratory infection right about the time I had chemo, but I didn't know if it was the chemo or what the heck because I'm receiving a couple new drugs--so sick to say the least. The good news is I woke up today with renewed energy. I'm better! I mean, really better, like I woke up from a bad dream, and here is this beautiful world that I love so much, and I'm so amazed and proud that my body has this amazing ability to heal itself. It really humbles me that we are so amazingly made!! I am also so blessed and thankful to be covered in your prayers and love. I feel every single one of them, I promise, and am doing the same for all of you!

Can't believe this was a year ago already!! Ohhh, and the healing my little body has done since then!! That week was nothing compared to what was to come, and WE did it!! So grateful to everyone who raises me up daily!! … It's no wonder I have the ability to heal and move forward!! It's all thanks to your loving prayers and support!! Have a great day, friends. I love you all!!

January 27, 2020

I've had a fantastic day! For no reason except the sun was shining, and I feel so much better!! As usual, chemo kicked my ass for almost a week, but I didn't fight it, just allowed myself to be sick and lazy, letting this life-saving medicine do its work. I wish we had better options for meds, and I believe they are coming, but for now, we fight this battle with what options are, and I feel really grateful for these days and the week to come cuz these are my days. These are not cancer's days. They are mine!! And, I will seize them!! Carpe Diem, everyone!! I love you! Thank you for holding me up!

February 1, 2020

> Getting your shit
> together requires a
> badass level of honesty.
> It's about facing you're
> the only one that's been
> holding you back this
> whole time!
>
> @WILDWOMANBUSINESSHOOD

I think I have learned this lesson over and
over and over. Life gives us a bunch of
adversities where we feel confused and lost,
trying to deal with the drama and get our shit
together with people, jobs, bills, illness—geez.
I have looked in the mirror so many times,
and I always come to this, if I am responsible,
I own it. If I'm not, it's not mine to own.

February 6, 2020

Today marks three years since my first surgery
for colon cancer. It seems so much longer
than that!! I went all the way back on
Facebook to that time in 2017 and saw
nothing from myself about having surgery or
my diagnosis or at my first misdiagnosis.
Weird huh? I never said the word CANCER.
Why was I being so private about it when I
have been so verbal the last couple years? I'm
thinking, I didn't want to worry my family and
friends. I wanted to be the strength for them
in my own storm!! Was gonna prove that I
was going to beat this thing silently and
without complaint! Boy, has that changed!! I
still don't complain much, but what I do
know is, I'm glad I reached out for prayers
and support. I'm glad that I tell my story now
in hopes that it reaches others in a positive
way! My hope is that my story can encourage
others to find strength in their own storms
and to know just how much they are cared for
and loved by the One who made us. I
couldn't have done these last three years
without the prayers and loving support of my

Facebook family, my friends, my family!!
Thank you!! I love you all!!

February 10, 2020

Hello, Hi, my name is Toni, and I have awakened from my chemo slumber!! Lol. Boy these drugs stack up and I almost lost a whole week!! Yesterday was the first day I got my spunky self back!! I heard the birds chirping this morning and finally felt like ME!! I'm sooooooo grateful for these days, and the only reason I even tell you these things is that I hope to give hope to those going through this. There are good days after treatment. I promise!! And for those who love us, be patient. Don't' take it personally. You didn't do it and thank you for loving us! Today, I am Warrior Strong and looking forward to a great week!!

February 18, 2020

Me today!! Surgery again tomorrow, probably
the least invasive surgery I've had to date, but
I'm having more anxiety about this than all of
them put together. Maybe that's why—
because there have been so many memories
of pain, recover, and dependence on others.
Ugh! They say PTSD with this damn disease
is real, and I'm here to tell ya, they, whoever
they are is right!

February 19, 2020

Surgery went well, removed that golf-ball sized friend of mine forever I hope!! Plenty of pain right now, but I'm planning on recovering quick and being ready to move, move, move by the first day of spring!! Thanks for the good thoughts and prayers!! I felt every one!!

February 28, 2020

Hahaha! This made me laugh!! Been a rough couple weeks, but I'm feeling much better!!

March 2, 2020

For real!! I struggle with this on a regular basis. This disease and I have an emotional love/hate relationship. LOL. The drugs and disease want to steal my hope and keep me in the dark feeling a victim, and boo hoo for me. I HATE that!! I feel so blessed that I am able to put those days behind me every two weeks, raise myself up, and be who I am. That's a gift from my Maker, and I am truly grateful!! I LOVE that!! So much of life and any chronic disease or bad situation brings us to this point. I choose to grow, rethink, and find my gratitude!! Thank you, warriors, for always holding me up!! I love you!

March 18, 2020

Just thinking tonight how grateful I am. Yes, grateful! Giving my glory to God today! I, of course, have been feeling the anxiety of this virus thing. I was feeling a little down because my good week is being spent isolating myself because I'm fighting an infected port, a big sore on my face that doesn't want to heal— blah, blah, blah. I have had so many people reach out to me wanting to help. I don't need much right now, but words can't describe how loved I feel!! Really. Thank youall!! I snuck a trip to tractor supply today cuz my friend, Louie, needs to eat. Had to purchase a little starter flower kit. If I can't get out and see the beauty, I'm gonna grow it!! Hope you all are well and safe. Love you bunches.

April 6, 2020

After a good discussion with my doc, I have decided not to do chemo for six weeks and then recheck. I'm feeling good and feel like my body is in healing mode! I know I will have some treatments for the rest of my live, but today I'm gonna relax and enjoy the fact that I'm not sick!! Corrie ten Boom was a brave, courageous, tenacious woman!! I strive to be like her. Keep me in your prayers, and I will keep you all in mine!!

April 7, 2020

LOOK what I found on my porch!! All cleaned up and ready for spring!

April 7, 2020

Here's your pink moon, Momma! I'll let you share the story!

Mary Whitaker

Last year, on Good Friday, Toni had just undergone a horrendous cancer surgery and was in ICU. As I sat in the recliner beside her bed, praying that she would be okay, I heard her say, "Mom, I don't want to bother you, but come here and look at the pink moon."

Remembering this makes me cry with thankfulness, and I will always wait for the pink moon!

Mary Whitaker
I`m sure you did Toni!
That`s who you are

4y   Like   Reply   3 😊👍

Toni Brown
Mary Whitaker I think it
was HOPE for us all! And
the people waiting in the
waiting room or hotel..I
don't remember much
after that but I'm grateful
I remembered this
moment!!

4y   Love   Reply   3 😊👍

April 10, 2020

I mentioned before that Good Friday was a special day for me always, but the last one was extra special, so here goes, I became a warrior. Good Friday. The day Jesus died for me. This was the day I knew pain in the most unadulterated way. This was the day I knew fear for my life. This was the day I felt grief for the people I may leave behind.

And, this was the day that, because he died for me, I WAS saved. I became a warrior on this day, walking into battle with Him by my side. With faith and hope and love as my guide, my story is a testament to the fighters out there.

You're not alone. We fight together. Stay warrior strong!! Love you all!!

~

Toni wrote this about her experience after the massive surgery that she had gone through on that Good Friday. Good Friday was always a day that she seemed to be so very aware of and sad for the pain Jesus suffered (and also the suffering of others). I am sure it was Christ's gift to her. It drew her very close to Him. May God draw us all close to Him today and always. Happy Easter.

−Mary

April 28, 2020

I'm missing my prayer warriors!! I'm a couple months now out of chemo, and I feel pretty good—getting things accomplished—doing work I haven't been able to do in a long time! It was a good time for a break. Sometimes fear sets in. Did I do the right thing? Am I playing games with myself and this disease? Probably. But, I have enjoyed this time. I promise I will get back in the chemo game if I have to. But, for now, HOPE is what I cling to!! I truly love you all and am praying everyone is safe and happy!

May 17, 2020

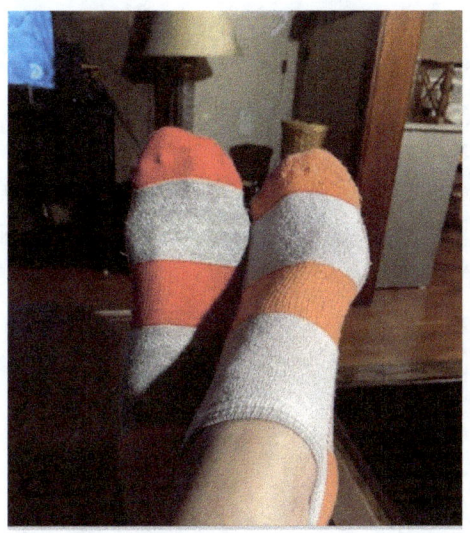

And, in other news, I'm sure I have a matching pair like this somewhere!! Geez!! LOL. Blood work and doc appointment tomorrow. Feeling a little stressed, but it will be whatever it is. I have enjoyed my time off, and for that, I am grateful.

May 18, 2020

Okay, gang. The news was kinda as I expected. CT scan on Tuesday, and chemo will more than likely start on Wednesday. Wish I knew how to beat this damned disease, but you know I will soldier on! Thank you for all of your support! At least I have one more week of freedom!!

May 24, 2020

And there is always a little, I know I'm being protected in a great way. Everywhere I go, I love the cross at the end of the road.

May 27, 2020

OH MY GOODNESS, gang of warriors!! My scan showed no evidence of disease…I'm jumping for joy that I could give my mother this news on her birthday!! I do have some fluid around my lung that we need to keep an eye on and a tiny blood clot in the same lung that we will treat with meds, but for today, this is the best news ever!! Happy Birthday MOM!! And warriors, your thoughts, prayers, and hope for me have surrounded me with greatness! God is good!!

June 4, 2020

Today, I spent some time at St. Francis Hospital like my body likes to do now and again, lol, I'm still on a chemo break but have been struggling with some fluid around my lung, so we took it out. Weird experience, and I've had more of a lay down than I thought. But, it's okay!! What I want to say is I sure love those people!! Debbie in radiology held my hand, calmed my fears, and talked me through it! I hope to meet her again! Not one mention of what's going on in society right not—no sobering faces because of "these trying times," totally focused on me and my comfort and for that, I will be eternally grateful! If you wanna be like anyone, be like Debbie!! I could tell she loved me and didn't even know me.

June 11, 2020

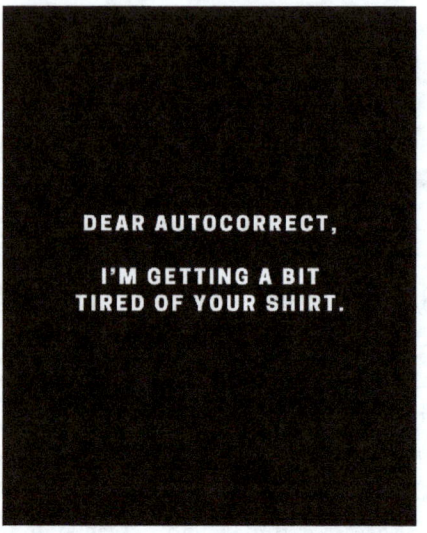

Just this tonight! Because I'm at a loss for words, and this gave me a chuckle. I'm tired of all the shirts too!!

June 23, 2020

Front row parking and a beautiful message from my friends at Milk & Honey!! Maintaining my independence is very important!! Thanks for the boost this morning!

July 4, 2020

Off my front porch!! God's promise and my American flag—how fitting for this day!! God bless America and all of you!

July 10, 2020

So, warriors, we took a BUNCH of fluid
yesterday, but my lung didn't re-expand, so,
I'm still suffering. I'm really disappointed to
say the least. I have lost so much mobility and
strength due to this. Feeling really lost with no
plan. I know I have to be my own advocate in
this battle, and I will, but I pray for strength
to fight, and I'm asking for you all to—geez,
I'm a hot mess, and that's not normal for me
is it? I think it's the no-plan thing or the no-
energy thing, or the no-ability thing. I'm
whining, I know, but damn, this is the shits!
Thanks for always being here for me and
raising me up!!

July 17, 2020

Okay, here's the scoop. The fluid was full of cancer cells, of course, cuz that's what this damned disease does. I really was praying that it was just a little lung issue that we can fix, and I could be cancer free for a while. Sometimes, I like to hang out in denial, so I can enjoy the time I have here, and I have, really for months! So, given the choice to keep fighting with chemo and a pulmonologist for comfort, guess what I chose? I'm a warrior, and quitting is just not in my nature. It would go against everything in my nature to give up! So, we get back in the game of chemo next week—someday, if they ever call me back. And pray always for another day to share with my loves and you all!! Wish I had better news, but I'm okay. I promise! My faith is strong, and my strength comes from HIM!

July 26, 2020

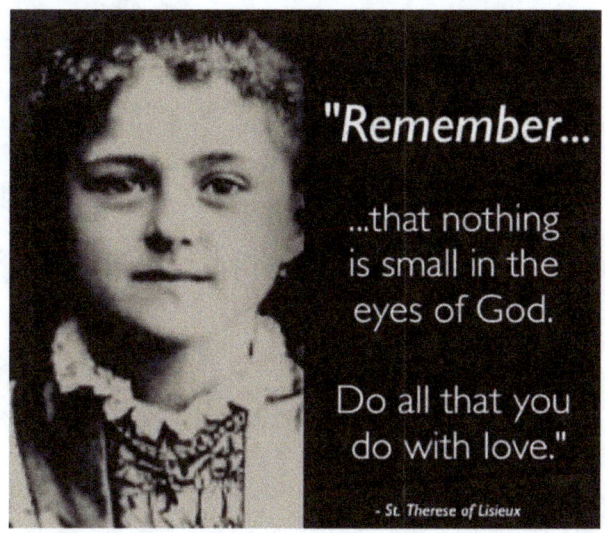

"Remember...

...that nothing
is small in the
eyes of God.

Do all that you
do with love."

- St. Therese of Lisieux

Love her!

August 15, 2020

Sorting through papers and found this. I don't even remember writing it or when, but it gave me a huge chuckle!! Stay with it, you deep thinkers out there.

If poetry could read my thoughts,

The words would flow in an organized way.

Not the jumble that I feel today.

If poetry could read my thoughts,

There would be words and inspiration

That touched your hearts.

If poetry could read my thoughts,

It would tell of sadness and loss,

Even anger and pain.

If poetry could read my thoughts,

It would tell of frustration and weight.

If poetry could read my thoughts,

It would tell of acceptance and grace.

I must have gotten way distracted or tired, the last line is:

If poetry could TALK,

It would say "All deep thinkers,

NEED TO GO TO BED!

Not all words are inspired, and sometimes we have to slap ourselves in the head.

August 28, 2020

So, the last week or month or two have been the shits. That's the only way I can explain chemo. On top of having a tube in my chest that has to be tended to every other day, I now have an infected port site. Will be having that surgically moved to the other side next Thursday. I always want to wait until the problems are resolved to post—until I wrap my brain around the plan and can find the HOPE in it. And, that's what I'm doing now. I promise, I'm not complaining. All of these things are necessary to continue to fight this battle! My hope in these posts is for the reader, my prayer warriors, to know that no matter what, and I mean, no matter what, as long as you live and breathe, there is nothing you can't survive. Yes, I get depressed and worried, but I'm here to tell you, I refuse to live there. My heart can't stay there. Tomorrow is always a new day, and I choose to seize that! Love you all so much! Carpe Diem!! Pray for me, and I'll pray for you!!

HAPPINESS

Happiness. That illusive word and feeling that seems always in the distance. Like the track dog chasing the rabbit, but it's always out of reach. We can see happiness, but we can never catch it.

We try to fill ourselves with things. More money. Bigger toys. People. Gambling. Drugs, Searching, searching, searching for some THING to make us happy. Do those things work? Maybe for an instant, then it's gone, and we are left searching some more. These THINGS do not have the power to make us happy.

I believe that we are wired to find happiness in love. In the giving and sharing of ourselves with the world. Happiness lies dormant inside all of us, waiting for us to let go of the thinking that THINGS bring joy. I believe that only love can fill our hearts and souls to overflowing. Love of self. Love for others. Love for the world we live in, and love for our God, the One who made us!

I rejoice in that knowledge today and plan to keep my eyes wide open! I don't want to miss the happiness within my reach.

Prayer: Dear Lord, I pray today for you to continue guiding me to the feelings of peace and happiness. Help me to let go of thoughts and feelings that get in the way of that happiness. Amen.

FACEBOOK

September 13, 2020

There are a few of you who remember me when!! Oh, these trips down memory lane are bringing back some fond memories.

November 13, 2020

Marching through quicksand is exhausting, but I sure have been shown what I'm made of these last few weeks. Had a little medicine break to get loads of work done and much accomplished! Already dreading getting back in the cancer fighting game, but I know I must. Next week, we focus on health and finding peace in the game of life! Have a great weekend, friends! I love you all!

November 24, 2020

I don't know how to be anything
other than intense.

I don't know how to experience
without feeling too much and
thinking too much.

I don't know how to sit still and quiet
my mind and just be.

I am always searching, always
questioning, struggling to find the
meaning of everything.

I am passionate, and I am deep, and
even if I am misunderstood, I am
finally okay with that.

AUTHOR UNKNOWN

Don't know who wrote this, but it sure spoke
to me!! I am all these things and so much
more, and I'm finally okay with that.

December 7, 2020

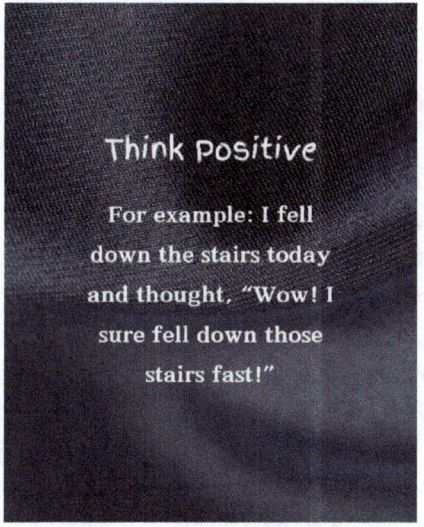

I mean, how else would you look at it? Anyone who knows me well has seen me fall down a time or two for one reason or another. Gotta stay positive. Life is a slippery slope!!

January 9, 2021

He speaks the truth. It's our soul that needs filled. It's that emptiness that we feel even when things are going well. It's the searching, searching, searching to fill this void. Nothing can fill this but faith in our Father and His Son. I know that because I've walked this and felt the love. Believe it or not, it's up to you, but there is peace here. There is love here. No thing or person can fulfill this but a relationship with the One who made us! I truly hope this for every human being on this planet! I love you, warriors, and so does HE!

January 13, 2021

My journey today! Love you, warriors!

As I wander around looking for the light,
My mind wants to be filled with the emotion
of fright.

The voice said, Keep looking. It's just up
ahead"
You must trust the direction you're led."

"Are you sure?" I said. "This place looks
awful bleak.
It's cold out there, and I don't' have enough
heat."

The voice said, "Keep moving, dear one.
I promise I will warm you with my sun."

"Yes," I said, although I forgot a scarf,
it's not so bad as I move away from the dark."

I was warmed completely, and my senses were
engaged.
Sights, sound, and beauty permeated my
brain.

The voice said, "Now, isn't that better?
You've been warmed by my Spirit, and we will
always do this together."

Toni Brown

January 13, 2021

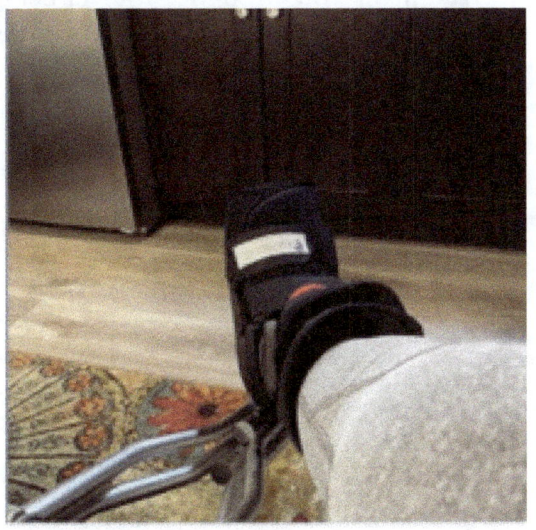

And in true Toni fashion, thirty seconds after I posted that lovely story, I tried to stand up, leg was asleep and got tangled in my Uggh boots and went all the way down. Thank the good Lord, the only thing broken is my ankle! It's another minor set back as it is my driving foot. I told a friend earlier that I usually end up writing what the future me needs to hear. Happened again today! Fair amount of pain, but we've done that before, and I truly am okay! And thank you, Mom, for forever being my hero!

January 23, 2021

Warrior strong!!

January 29, 2021

Update:scan looks relatively stable. Bloodwork looks good, so we just keep doing what we are doing for now. Thanks for all the prayers. I feel every one of them!

CT and bloodwork today. Doctor visit and chemo tomorrow. Scan anxiety is really bad this time. Maybe I don't' trust this oral chemo. Maybe I'm just waiting for the other shoe to fall. It's such a mental game, but I just now remembered the CT tech had to move my necklace because I forgot to take it off. She said, "Is that St. Perigrine?"

I said, "Yes, but who's the other?" because I change them up sometimes.

She said, "St. Michael."

I said, "Those two are my warriors." We left it at that, but I know they are fighting for me, and I'm surrounded by their protection, one way or the other!! I'll keep you posted. Pray for me and I'll pray for you!! Love you, warriors!

February 1, 2021

I don't want this hoody and wouldn't wear it because I'm always hoping sick doesn't show on my face, and cancer doesn't define me. But this says it all in the "I'm fine" world for anyone fighting any disease or other disorder. Stay strong. I know you and I feel you! Much love!

February 13, 2021

Got a few words of wisdom from my dad
tonight. Yes, it's cold, and yes, he's hauling
wood in by the loads, and he's not
complaining about it. He said that neither is
my mom. It's in the cold that things break.
I've been aching and paining and worrying
and maybe complaining in my mind, but these
two parents of mine have again shown me
that ALL is well, and that is where I get my
strength. I love you both!! Thank you!!

February 26, 2021

I'll take this view every day of my life!! No filter, just the beauty of nature right off my front porch!!

March 6, 2021

I've been trying to come up with words to talk about Colon Cancer Awareness month. Someone told me last night to tell my story, but it's longggg, and most of you know it. I don't want you to relive my struggles or pain, but I do want you to NEVER ignore a symptom, such as irritable bowel or pain and pressure or bleeding. I did those things for years, moving through life and not taking care of myself. It's treatable, preventable, but has to be caught in its early stages! Please, please, please! It's not embarrassing, and it can be deadly!! If your symptomatic before age fifty, push your doc. It's happening to thirty-somethings every day! Thanks for reading. I may have used this photo to get your attention. Now, here's a photo of my front porch!! I have zero energy, but I accomplished this today.

March 16, 2021

Just a little update. My maintenance may be coming to an end. It's looking like I may be throwing my hat in the big ring again in the next few weeks. I don't have many details, just my tumor markers rising and a couple under the skin little lumps causing me some pain. CT scan in three weeks, and I'll know more. I knew this was temporary cuz for me, cancer is not going away. But make no mistake. This photo represents the strength of an amazing beast, and I plan to continue fighting.

March 31, 2021

Yesterday, I was reminded that maybe I need a new hobby. It's so my nature to appreciate the beauty in this world, and I'm gently reminded that no person, place, or thing can give me more satisfaction than trying to capture nature and to write about the peace it brings me! Happy Wednesday, friends! I love you bunches!

April 2, 2021

Remember I said we are wrapped in Jesus's
ever-loving arms? Just got a call because they
didn't want me to worry about my scan this
morning. NO new findings. In fact, the tumor
on my tummy is shrinking! I get to stay on the
maintenance meds, and that, I can function
with!! PRAISE THE LORD!! This is
definitely Good Friday. I couldn't wait to tell
you all!! I love you! Happy Easter!

April 11, 2021

I took this photo the other day. I was in awe of this tiny ladybug. She's just doing what she does. She has a purpose, although I'm not totally sure what that is. That is so me sometimes. Moving through life is just doing what I do. Sometimes my purpose seems insignificant, then I slap myself in the forehead, straighten out the self-talk and keep moving! Every creature on this planet is beautifully and wonderfully made, including us humans, although we wonder sometimes. But God doesn't make mistakes, and we are right where we are supposed to be. Hope you all had a great weekend!! Love you bunches!!

April 14, 2021

Excerpt from something I wrote a long time ago, reminding me the words I say to myself are the most important. Enjoy or scroll. I just feel like sharing.

"Choose Your Words

Words fascinate me.

The way individual words put together create meaning. Express thought. Give pleasure or pain. We use words in every aspect of our lives. All of our thoughts come in sentences, all are dreams are created by the way we put our words together. The way that we speak to ourselves has a strong impact on our beliefs, actions, and emotions. I've found so many inspirations in the words of others. They have a gift. Self talk is so important as is how we speak to others."

Not in its entirety because I don't' want to bore you. Stay strong loved ones!

April 15, 2021

Because if you keep
hope alive,
it will keep you alive.

Hope. My favorite word with so many meanings. Is it a prayer? Is it a wish? We use it daily in our everyday language. We hope for new jobs, relationships, health, wealth, and on and on. To me, Hope goes with faith and my plan and purpose on this earth—to walk in a way on this planet that ultimately leads to me spending eternity with my Maker. Shedding the hope of things completely out of my control, which is most things, has so much made me a more peaceful person. Life is a fragile balance, and as St. Francis said, "Lord, make me an instrument of your peace." There is so much HOPE in those words!

April 25, 2021

What do I do pre chemo and bloodwork day?
Make sure I have something to look forward
to and tend to all summer long!! And, of
course, purple petunias are my favorite.

April 26, 2021

Mom, pink moon!! ICU, remember this two years ago? Brought tears to my eyes. We are so blessed!!

May 4, 2021

HaHa!! That's for sure!! All is well, folks. Now they are browbeating me into radiation tomorrow. That doesn't really fit in my schedule, but I guess I'll go. Only five treatments, twenty minutes a day, so I'll be done next Tuesday!! Easy breezy! I got this. Say goodbye, little tumors!!

May 17, 2021

This was me today—doesn't happen very often, but sometimes I get DONE—done with cancer, done with waging war all the time, done being in constant fight mode. The past couple weeks, I've had five radiation treatments and a shot in my shoulder. I've been scanned, MRI'd, sonogrammed, I've had a mask on more than I haven't, and an infusion of chemo today, which took way too long. Don't get me wrong. I'm grateful for the care that I get, and I love the people immensely.

May 23, 2021

Sometimes to clear my head, I take a little drive to the Wakarusa River. I have memories of camping and fishing on these banks. I had to get out and smell the smells and feel the feels and know that although the river is up, it will subside, and nature always takes its course in the most beautiful of ways. It truly connects me with the one who loves me every time! I hope everyone had a great weekend and wish you all an amazing week!

VISUALIZING

Since we can't manipulate time, and we are searching for happiness or at least peace in our souls, we could use our imaginations to visualize ourselves elevated above the dramas of our lives. So many thoughts weigh us down, thoughts of illness, money, pain, fear of losing a friend or loved one. I imagine putting all the worries in balloons one at a time and holding them like a big bouquet, and now we are going to LET them go!

Loneliness   Fear

Worry   Anxiety   Stress

Fatigue   Pain   Loss

Frustration   Anger

Resistance   Sadness

Expectation

Giving these feelings names today, so we don't have to be tethered to them. We no longer have to rush or push or manipulate or fret or fuss or fight. We can just release and wait for the One who made us to line our lives up just right.

Prayer: Dear Lord, you own the scissors. Please cut the cord. Amen.

FACEBOOK

June 5, 2021

She was tired.

No one could see the level of tired.
They saw the outside.
The one giving, smiling, showing up.
And yet inside, she felt the fatigue.
The tired of trying to keep up.
The tired of agendas.
The tired of worries.
But she kept on.

She kept on giving and loving.
She kept on hoping.
She kept on showing up. She knew her
giving mattered.
She pushed forward.
Out of love.

Even in the tired.

Someone on the colon cancer site posted this, and I could relate on every level. It was written by a mom, but every chronic disease warrior can relate.

June 22, 2021

My thoughts tonight as scan anxiety sets in. sometimes, you have to surrender to a fight in order to win the war!! In other words, let the small stuff go—the worries, the anxiety, the fear. I've been fighting a lot lately for one reason or another—regressing mentally, hashing out old crap, feeling lost in who I am. This cancer battle and the world itself will do that to me if I let it, and some days, I just let it. Regrouping tonight. Putting on my armor and praying with my whole heart that I can stay in this phase of treatment a while longer. I'll keep you posted on the results, but if you would pray for my, I will pray for you. Love you so much warriors!!

June 24, 2021

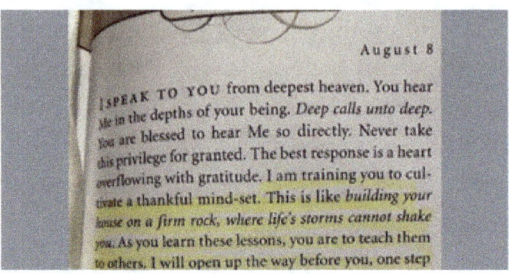

Sometimes I can't hear him,

Or I can't pray.

Life or fear,

Or the need to control truly gets in His way,

but my heart is pure, or I HOPE it is anyway.

Kinda grateful tonight.

That he leads my way.

I am a work in progress,

For that I know is true.

But

I am a willing servant,

For the One who loves me so.

**Just playing with the words and looking for inspiration. This little book never fails me. And yes, I know the date is wrong.

June 28, 2021

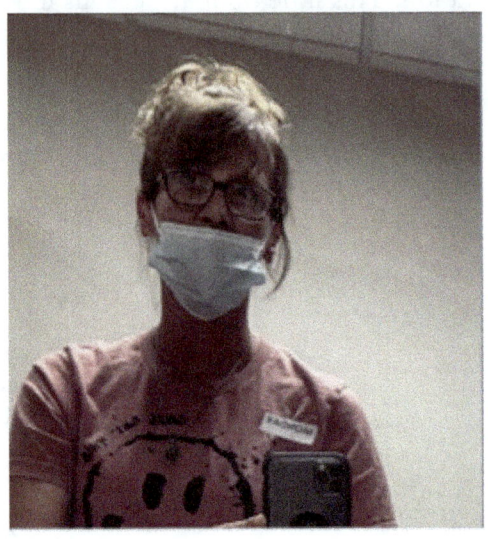

Not too good a selfie, lol, but I wanted to keep you all updated on my visit today. There has been some tumor growth, and my numbers are sneaking up, not much, but just a little every time. But we got a good plan. My blood work is great, and I've gained a good amount of weight, so we are going to rescan and do some biopsies for new genetic testing in six weeks. There really isn't any point to removing these tumors as this disease doesn't work that way.

June 29, 2021

July 3, 2021

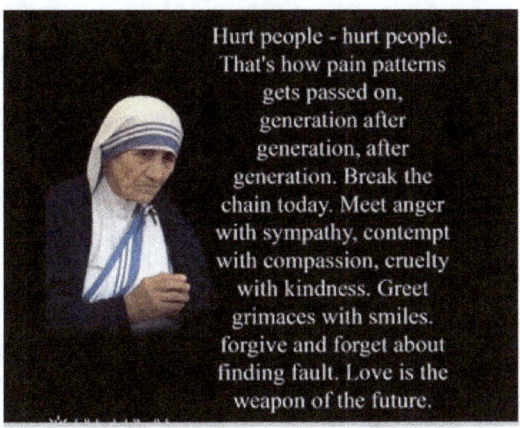

Hurt people - hurt people. That's how pain patterns gets passed on, generation after generation, after generation. Break the chain today. Meet anger with sympathy, contempt with compassion, cruelty with kindness. Greet grimaces with smiles. forgive and forget about finding fault. Love is the weapon of the future.

I wish I had her calmness of spirit, her understanding, her faith!! I try, but geez, some days the world truly wears on me. It's noisy and hateful, sometimes dark and destructive—the news, the attitudes, the drama. The traffic, the sadness, the beggars on the street, it's so much harder to breathe Hope in this world than it used to be, or maybe I'm getting tired. Dear Jesus, give me strength!

July 10, 2021

And these moments, I know that God is good. I feel His beauty and presence, and it calms me to my very soul. I am so safe with the One who loves me!

July 15, 2021

Tomorrow I got in my own cancer game again. Got a call last week, and radiation oncologist wants me seen by a lady who has no answers. LOL. And has ordeed staging, for what I don't know! I thought me and doc C had a plan for biopsies around Labor Day. Worrisome to say the least because something is happening without my knowledge. I trust her immensely, so I'm just gonna go like I always do and ask for prayers from you all. Please raise this chickie up cuz this damned rollercoaster is wearing me out!! Thank you so much guys. Feeling really raw and edgy and looking for my strength.

July 19, 2021

This is tough sometimes, but who I strive to be always.

August 7, 2021

THE MOST PAINFUL TEARS
ARE NOT THE ONES THAT
FALL FROM YOUR EYES AND
COVER YOUR FACE.

THEY'RE THE ONES THAT FALL
FROM YOUR HEART AND
COVER YOUR SOUL.

Author Unknown

We all know these tears. If you're struggling tonight, I'll pray for you if you pray for me. Love you!!

August 9, 2021

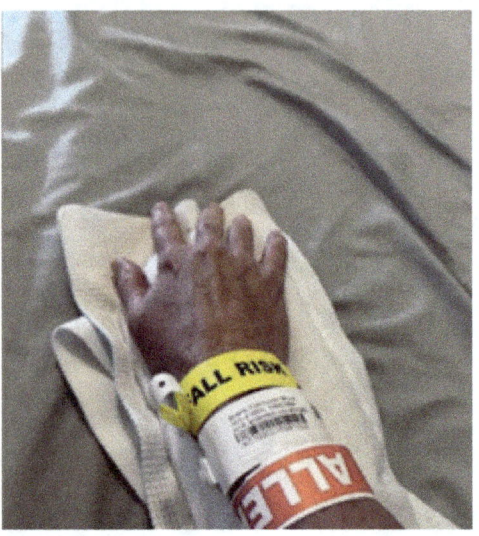

My choice of jewelry today!! Everything went well. Didn't actually biopsy the lung as it's been there for a while. Went for some newer tumor tissue under my sternum. Easy breezy. No problem. Thank you, friends. Your prayers helped me climb this mountain today! Now to rest and move through the rest of the week.

August 9, 2021

From Running4:

Please join us in sending love and strength to our friend Toni Brown as she prepares for an important week!

"So Monday begins a week of surgical biopsies to a tumor in my right lung. More scans and so on. Hoping to get a good chemo plan, so we can knock this horrible crap in the dirt once again. Feeling pretty depleted as I also have been dealing with a bad bout of colitis for a couple weeks that required a trip to the ER. Cancer caused inflammation, and it is so very painful. I'm gonna ask you all to raise me up and join me in trusting that God has me right where I am supposed to be…wrapped up in His loving arms. I've got my armor on but I'm having some trouble raising my sword! I know your prayers will get this job done. Thank you all! I love you so! I'll keep you posted.

August 11, 2021

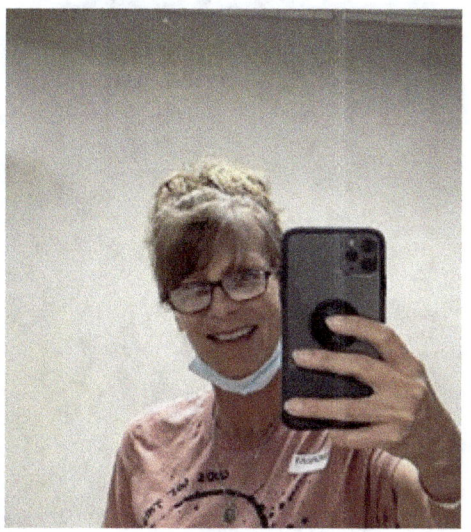

More phone than face, but I was rockin' my
favorite shirt, and I love how the hospital
always tells me what day it is.

August 13, 2021

Look, it's Friday. Scan and blood work today, and my shirt reminds me to be KIND as all the staff at St. Francis Cancer Center. I sure do love them.

August 17, 2021

My little buddies posing for change. I sure do love them.

August 20, 2021

Praying for healing…for myself…for my loves…for my fellow warriors! May we experience all the healing love that He truly has in store for us.

August 20, 2021

Ominous. Good thing we battered down the hatches. ☹ We will be picking up tree limbs again tomorrow.

August 21, 2021

I'm actually weeping over this loss…so many memories of that amazing trip!! Last minute airport find. It's been my favorite since. Damned neuropathy. Hands don't work—such a klutz.

August 23, 2021

Good morning! I thought maybe I should update from all of my last week appointments and what decisions I have made regarding my health.

The last six weeks have been really rough with unmanageable pain, constant colitis, scans, biopsies, and doc visits.

It's been A LOT of running in circles for not much result.

I was supposed to start chemo last week, but I said no!

Not forever no, but not until I get some of these other things under control. Chemo causes colitis, and I already have that. I don't dare let that get any worse, so I'm going to be seeing a gastro doc to see if I can get help with stabilizing this. Nutrition is a big deal, and right now, I'm not getting much.

We did a biopsy on a tumor under my sternum, hoping to get good genetic testing for a more targeted direct therapy. They didn't get enough tissue. Again. I have asked to be referred to the colon cancer specialist at KU Med who we have worked with in the past. Hopefully, that will be soon. Still waiting on that appointment and feeling hopeful that we can get some kind of answers as to why I am in so much distress!

I am no stranger to pain, but these last few weeks have knocked me on my butt!! I have started a stronger pain medication, which I don't love. I hate to trade my brain for pain, but right now, I have no choice. So, if you reach out, and I'm STUPID, that's why. Lol.

I've been cocooned up in my little house, trying to stay cozy and relaxed until I get a good plan—again letting go of all the drama and frustrations of this and staying focused on a good treatment plan. That plan is coming. I know God's got this. I just have to patiently wait for the timing of everything to fall into place! Love you all. Thanks for raising me up!! I'll keep you posted along the way. Pray for me please, and I will pray for you!!

August 25, 2021

A great big Happy Anniversary to my amazing parents!! Thank you both for being the amazing people that you are!! Here's to many more!

September 1, 2021

The sun kept its beauty all to itself tonight,
not flowing into clouds or rain, so beautiful,
but it looks like it doesn't belong there. I
swear I didn't fake it.

September 2, 2021

Grace is like a blanket
of hope that covers
you at night when you
think you don't have
what it takes to get up
in the morning.

CAROLINE MYSS

Such comforting words!

September 4, 2021

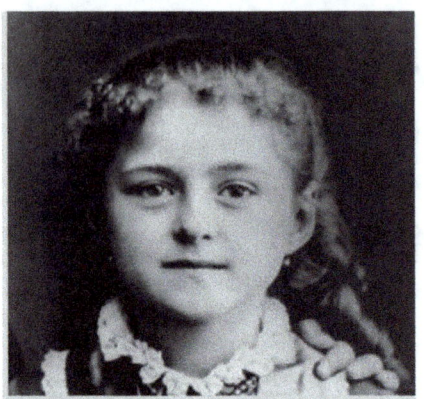

"Oh, how sweet is the way of love!
Oh, how I wish to always do the
will of God with no restraints.

St. Thérèse

I was reminded of this beautiful saint today,
so I spent some time reading her words again.
She has been a great inspiration to me for as
long as I can remember, and I find so much
comfort in her sweet faith. May I strive to
mimic her little ways in all the things that I do
and say!!

September 10, 2021

September 10, 2021

Me and my momma have had a big week! It's
Friday and the last of many appointments!
We're tired, or at least I am, but we're getting
some answers and hopefully will be able to
share a plan with you all once the docs put
their heads together! Keep raising us up
warriors cuz we need all the strength we can
muster! This woman is my ROCK, and I truly
couldn't do any of this without her!!

P.S. I LOVE YOU, MOM!!!

HOPE

To truly understand hope, I think we have to have felt hopeless. You know, that overwhelming feeling of despair. Hopelessness is such a devastating emotion, and I try not to go there. I have though. Many times. I have put my head in my hands and wept with sorrow over this situation or that one.

Hope is a hard word to understand. It's a feeling that niggles around in the back of our brains, allowing us to be pulled out of our misery. It's the *glimmer of hope*. It's *the light at the end of the tunnel*. It's my mantra of *This too shall pass*, repeated over and over until I believe it. It does pass, doesn't it? Think about last week, last month, last year, all the way back to whatever devastated us in the first place , and it's over. It's gone. Tomorrow really is a new day filled with excitement and joy over whatever is to come.

Hope is not only a feeling but an attitude. A way to perceive life, a way to walk in this world and share it with others. Hope gives us the ability to want and the patience to wait for it. Hope gives us courage when we are facing hardship and the unknown. Hope gives us strength to keep moving forward, no matter what.

Even if we don't know the outcome of where hope will take us, it's the faith and knowledge that it will be better than where we are today.

My ultimate goal with hope in my heart is Eternity, in heaven with the One who made us. My hope comes from Him, the rescuer, the redeemer, the almighty. Let's wait with that feeling for the coming of a new day.

Prayer: With the gratitude of Hope in my heart, I pray, Psalm 130:5. I wait for the Lord; my whole being waits, and in His word I put my Hope. Amen.

FACEBOOK

September 27, 2021

From Running4
#running4Toni

"I honestly can't even put into words what this last few weeks have looked like, so I'm not going to. Just want you all to know that I'm working on getting better, managing pain and restarting chemo—round two coming Friday!

This poem is a thank you to all my warriors, each and every one of you! Your thoughts, prayers, and actions literally gave me hope in what was a dark and scary situation. I am truly the most blessed girl on the planet to have all of you in my life. I love you so!!!

FINDING HOPE
September 2021

I can't tell you about Hope
Until you know desperation.
The excruciating pain of
Sinking in quicksand.

I can't breathe.
I can't see.
I can't think.
I can't move.

I would run, run, run,
But there is nowhere to go.
Is this the end??
Or is there a glimmer of hope?

My view out of my window
when morning arrives,
I can feel the fresh breeze,
and my brain comes alive.
Oh, yes! I'm reminded
the quicksand is gone!
My warriors brought bricks
each day one by one
Piece by piece, they laid hope
that all is not lost.
Strength came in knowing
that I am THAT loved.

That's when He told me "Get out of my way.
It's not your job to save every day.
I am holding you up; let me worry and care.

My love can move mountains.
It's only your job to share."

What a relief I felt
as these words cleansed my soul.
What a gift I'd been given
worth way more than gold.

I walked in with fear and burden and weight
but I left with new hope of beauty and grace.
All that negative baggage,
it didn't come with me home.
I left it at the end of that garden's gate.

WORDS

Words fascinate me. The way individual words put together create meaning, express thoughts, give pleasure or pain. We use words in every aspect of our lives. All of our thoughts come in sentences. All of our dreams are created by the way we put words together.

The way that we speak to ourselves has a strong impact on our beliefs, actions, and emotions. Self-talk is the most important! The words we form in our heads identify us as individuals and how we perceive ourselves. And let's be honest, those words usually end up coming out of our mouths.

Are your first thoughts in the morning insecurity filled? Full of anxiety? Full of anger or disgust? Or why me? If so, that's how your day's going to go. Sorry, we will project those words and emotions all day long to everyone we come in contact with.

I try really hard not to think too much first thing in the morning. That's when the demons want to steal my brain. I've found that if I just sit and be quiet, breathe, read, write, and pray first, my thoughts will soon turn to positive self-talk, peaceful thoughts, and a much better day.

Journaling is a fantastic way to release negative emotions or to get yourself excited about something. Reading a daily meditation book is also a great way to find a better self-talk. Some of my greatest tools for self-healing have come out of authors who have very inspiring words. Those words are such a gift to me.

Prayer: Dear Lord, thank you for the comfort of the words of others. Thank you for allowing me to continue to strive and grow. I pray that whoever reads this will know that NO battle is too big to overcome if we choose to feel in our hearts the good words of others. Amen.

WORDS IN MY HEAD
6/2/2021

I woke up this morning
feeling covered with
dread.
Oh my, my, I have too
many words in my head.
Thoughts, feelings,
emotions all twisted in knots.
Time to get moving before these thoughts rot.

Off to my safe place, kind of
contemplative and blue,
looking for inspiration, as I
often do.
I met this nice fellow and said,
"How do you do?"

He was enjoying a snack of left behind Chex
Mix® covered in dew.

We said goodbye with a smile and wave,
and I realized right then, it was beauty I crave.

Moving along, I stopped at the fountain

I imagined the water
removing this
mountain,
cleansing my mind of
these worthless
thoughts in my head,
healing my spirit and removing the dread.

I've been challenging my
existence
with too many questions
why?
Am I a weed or a flower
in this game called life?

What is my purpose? Am I significant
enough?
Lord, this life's journey sure gets kind of
rough.

FINDING THE MAGIC

I've been searching, Dear Lord
since the day I was born,
to find the magic
I know you have shown.

I looked to the mountains.
I looked to the tide.
When I stopped searching,
I looked deep inside.

I found that within me,
You weren't trying to hide.
The magic's been flowing
through me all this time!

It's here in my heart
and my soul
and my mind.
What a journey it's been.

All the memories are there,
but my spirit's been guided
by the One who cares.

Rejoice in the mountains.
Play in the tide.

The search is over.
The magic's inside.

BELIEVE

Being

Ever prayerful and

a**L**ways

fa**I**thful

Even in the most

de**V**estating

tim**E**s of your life.

P.S. He loves you, and so do I!!!

Toni Brown

CIRCUS

My head is pounding with all this intrusion.
Why must there be so much
false and illusion?

Looking for real in the world all around me,
I get slight of hand,
and magicians surround me.

Tempt me not
to a place of darkness.
Let me rise to the task
and see truth where my heart is.

So many villains and evil court jesters
weigh on my mind until old wounds fester.

Tempt me not
to a place of disaster,
where money and lust and greed
are my master.

I served all of them once with
fear and resentment.
There was no joy,
no hope or contentment.

Clearer thoughts fill my head.
The time has come to send this circus to bed.
Goodnight villains, magicians, and jesters.
May we all find peace serving the One true
Master.

TIME

I've never really thought, until lately, how much we try to manipulate time. We want to speed it up when things are boring or we are looking forward to something. We really want to speed it up when we are distressed or grieving something. We don't want to feel what's happening to us. It hurts. We want it to go away.

We also want to slow down time. Especially when we are enjoying a moment, a situation or a thing. Sometimes we even want to stop time because we feel so peaceful and euphoric, freeze it and us in that moment forever. It feels good, and we want it to stay.

We are such creatures of avoiding pain, always looking for happiness and joy. What we don't realize is that there are lessons to be learned in the uncomfortable, painful moments. Life lessons! The ones we need to survive and grow, the lessons we need to nurture our soul.

We know that we cannot manipulate time, but all of the moments bring us what we need to become who we are meant to be.

Today, I will cherish all that time has given me. I will feel time and let it flow through me. Every moment is a gift and will not go unnoticed.

Prayer: Dear Lord, thank you for the gift of time. Help me to learn the lessons that time is teaching me. Help me to be open to all of the feelings, good and bad, that this gift of time will bring to me. Amen.

WAIT WITH ME

Wait with Me a while, and you will feel the
truth.
Lay down you tarnished sword.
Lay down your axe and shield.
Your wounds tell a story of your fight
to my glory.

Now it's time to surrender.
Surrender your loss.
Surrender your anger and hate.
Now is the time to lay down the fight.

If
you wait with Me a while, you will feel the
truth.
Peace, I want to give you.
Hope will be your norm.
Grace becomes your stature,
when you wait within My arms.
My love is everlasting, beyond all time and
space.
So, wait with Me a while, and you will see…
My face.

FACEBOOK

November 18, 2021

So looking forward to holidays with my family!!

And as

Individuals,

We become whole,

Seeing beauty through

A family lens,

Always brings us home!!

September 26, 2021

A little late on the daughter's day, but this is
MY Frankie, the beautiful I was blessed to
raise! So proud of her and all her sassy wit and
go get 'em attitude!! Love you bunches, Frankie
Brown!!

October 7, 2021

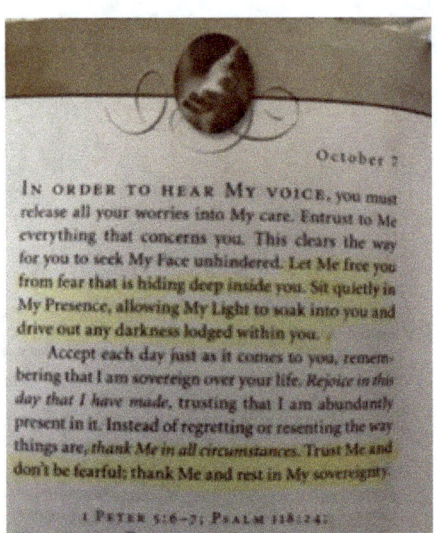

IN ORDER TO HEAR MY VOICE, you must release all your worries into My care. Entrust to Me everything that concerns you. This clears the way for you to seek My Face unhindered. Let Me free you from fear that is hiding deep inside you. Sit quietly in My Presence, allowing My Light to soak into you and drive out any darkness lodged within you.

Accept each day just as it comes to you, remembering that I am sovereign over your life. *Rejoice in this day that I have made,* trusting that I am abundantly present in it. Instead of regretting or resenting the way things are, *thank Me in all circumstances.* Trust Me and don't be fearful; thank Me and rest in My sovereignty.

1 PETER 5:6–7; PSALM 118:24;

Feeding my spirit with these comforting words. This little book always speaks to my soul!!

October 12, 2021

The colors are magical!

October 13, 2021

Coffee and convo with Louie! He says I have to go to chemo today. He's soooo bossy! Okay, Louie. I'm getting my Bad Asstra on the way!! Wish me well!!

October 21, 2021

Where are you this morning?
I'm waiting for you to arrive.
Sneaking glances at my window
to watch you open your sleepy eyes.

I can feel the daybreak creeping,
smell it in the morning breeze.
Yet, I believe you're being lazy
and don't want to come to me.

Big yawn for you this morning.
I see the clouds are in your way.
So, I will rest here ever more gently
waiting for you to start my day.

Toni Brown - 10/21

November 11, 2021

My favorite little cemetery in Berryton, honoring our veterans!! Thanks all you veterans, for your service!!

November 14, 2021

Still so real and true and explains a lot about our suffering!

Post from November 12, 2020

So good. So true.

> I would have pulled Joseph out. Out of that pit. Out of that prison. Out of that pain. I would have cheated nations out of the one God would use to deliver them from famine.

> I would have pulled David out. Out of Saul's spear-throwing presence. Out of the caves he hid away in. Out of the pain of rejection. I would have cheated Israel out of a God-hearted king.

> I would have pulled Jesus off. Off of the cross. Off the road that led to suffering and pain. Off the path that would mean nakedness and beatings, nails and thorns. I would have cheated the entire world out of a Savior. Out

of salvation. Out of an eternity filled with no more suffering and no more pain.

And oh, friend, I want to pull you out. I want to change your path. I want to stop your pain. But right now I know I would be wrong. I would be out of line. I would be cheating you and cheating the world out of so much good. Because God knows. He knows the good this pain will produce. He knows the beauty this hardship will grow. He's watching over you and keeping you in the midst of this. He's promising you that you can trust Him. Even when it all feels like more than you can bear.

So instead of trying to pull you out, I'm lifting you up. I'm kneeling before the Father and I'm asking Him to give you strength. To give you hope. I'm asking him to protect you and to move you when the time is right. I'm asking Him to help you stay prayerful and discerning. I'm asking Him how I can best love you and be a help to you. I'm believing He's going to use your life in powerful and beautiful ways. Ways that will leave your heart grateful and humbly thankful for this road you've been on.

Author Unknown

October 25, 2021

The deepest level of worshop is
praising God inspite of the pain,
thanking God during the trials,
trusting Him when we're tempted to
lose HOPE, and LOVING HIM when
he seems so distant and far away.

At my lowest, God is my hope.

At my darkest, God is my light.

At my weakest, God is my strength.

At my saddest, God is my comforter.

I wish I would have written this!! Praising,
thanking, and trusting Him every day of my
life!

October 27, 2021

To that one soul reading this. I know you're tired. You're fed up. You're so close to breaking, but there's strength within you, even when you feel weak.

I've been here many times lately but not today. This morning, I'm drinking coffee and making a plan to drive in the rain and spend the day with my cancer team, feeling grateful that I still have them and these drugs to keep me here with all of you. Thay are a huge part of my HOPE for a tomorrow and get me through today's medicine!! This will be number four of this cocktail of drugs, and I believe we have tweaked the meds enough to tolerate the side effects better this time—I HOPE. I lost track of how many total treatments I've had, and I get asked that a lot. Let's just say over seventy-five in the almost five years that we have battled this brute! It's doable cuz I'm doing it!! So, if you're feeling a bit lost today or over tired or fed up with life, please remember mindset is everything! Be brave—the pain will pass—do whatever it is you have to do to get through it and know you are not alone!! We all fight together!! Love you warriors!! Go be amazing!

December 6, 2021

Little boho Christmas tree with a vintage brooch I've been working on! I love piddling with these little pieces of fabric.

December 25, 2021

We did a little fun photo shoot with all the family in. Christmas jammies last night. Everyone participated, and it was fun!! Now I put the photos in a little book and gift it to everyone, and we have Christmas memories forever.

January 18, 2022

I received several *check on me* notes today and realized I haven't updated in a long time, and that's not very nice of me, is it? Things have been a little rough. I've been transitioning to hospice the last couple weeks because chemo has stopped working, and the pain was unbearable. This way, I get my pain managed and to let life finish doing the rest. I'll be around a while. Chemo for me at this point was doing more damage than good, and I'm so fine with this decision.

It's a lot, but once things settle down, I'll be back on Facebook finding the beauty in the world!! I love you all, and trust me when I say you are still raising me up! Please don't stop. I feel you prayers and your love, and what more could a girl need? Thank you for checking on me! I try to respond as much as I can!

PSALM 23 (KJV)

The Lord is my shepherd: I shall not want.
He maketh me to lie down in green pastures.
He leadeth me beside the still waters.
He restoreth my soul: he leadeth me in the
paths
of righteousness for his namesake. Yea,
though I walk through the valley of the
shadow of death, I will fear no evil for thou
art with me; thy rod and thy staff, they
comfort me.
Thou preparest a table before me in the
presence of mine enemies: thou anointest my
head with oil; my cup runneth over. Surely
goodness and mercy shall follow me all the
days of my life, and I will dwell in the house
of the Lord forever.

     This prayer/psalm has been rolling
around in my head for months. I think I
always associated it with death. Reading it

over and over, I believe my strength and hope are right here in these words, "I shall not want," and I never really have; my needs have always been met. I've been blessed beyond measure. "He restoreth my soul" every day with a newness different from yesterday. "Yea, though I walk through the valley of the shadow of death, I will fear no evil for though are with me." There is so much comfort in these words, knowing I'm not fighting this battle of life alone. I have a legion of warriors, both here and beyond, and look! He's already prepared the table with my enemy and anointed my head with oil. Again, I am protected and am not fighting alone. This is not a death prayer because, "surely goodness and mercy shall follow me all the days of my life." My hope is dwelling in the house of the Lord forever.

Toni died on March 14, 2022. She hated reading or hearing the statement, "They lost their battle with cancer." To her, this insinuated the cancer that had tried to steal everything from her had won. The thought of leaving all of us that loved her so was heartbreaking for her, but she knew that the pain of this ugly disease would be over and that she would soon be in the loving arms of the One who loved her best. Cancer has not won this battle. It could not steal her away from Eternal Love.

The morning after her death, in my mind, I could see her standing with her arms raised, yelling excitedly to me, "Look, Mom! No pain!" Yes, Toni, you had won the battle!

Wanting all of Toni's prater warriors to know, Mary wrote this final post.

March 15, 2022

Our warrior took off her shield and lay down her sword Monday evening (March 14, 2022) and went home to be with the One who loves her most, where it is safe and warm and pain free. Thank God that is over for her, but our hearts are breaking at the thought of living without her. Thank all of you for your prayers and love. She counted on them and knew she was blessed by all of you. ~ Mary Whitaker